Eager Street Academy #884
401 East Eager Street
Baltimore, MD 21202

HOW THE LEGISLATIVE BRANCH WORKS

BY MADDIE SPALDING

Published by The Child's World®
1980 Lookout Drive • Mankato, MN 56003-1705
800-599-READ • www.childsworld.com

ACKNOWLEDGMENTS
The Child's World®: Mary Swensen, Publishing Director
Red Line Editorial: Editorial direction and production
The Design Lab: Design

Photographs ©: Shutterstock Images, cover, 2, 16 (top), 16
(bottom), 21 (center), 21 (right), 21 (far right); Orhan Cam/
Shutterstock Images, 5; Andrew Harnik/AP Images, 7, 12;
J. Scott Applewhite/AP Images, 9; Red Line Editorial, 11;
National Archives and Records Association, 14; Howard Chandler
Christy, 15; Asia Glab/Shutterstock Images, 16 (middle); Brendan
Hoffman/Getty Images, 19; EdStock/iStockphoto, 20; Ingka D.
Jiw/Shutterstock Images, 21 (far left); Vector Pro/Shutterstock
Images, 21 (left)

COPYRIGHT © 2017 by The Child's World®
All rights reserved. No part of this book may be reproduced or
utilized in any form or by any means without written permission
from the publisher.

ISBN 9781503809062
LCCN 2015958459

Printed in the United States of America
Mankato, MN
June, 2016
PA02309

**On the cover: The U.S. Capitol Building is
located in Washington, DC. It covers more than
1.5 million square feet (139,300 sq m).**

TABLE OF CONTENTS

CHAPTER 1

WHAT IS THE LEGISLATIVE BRANCH?

What sort of rules do you have in your house? "Take out the trash." "Finish your homework before you watch TV." "Remember to wash the dishes." Maybe some of these sound familiar. You may not like doing these tasks. But someone has to do them. These kinds of rules are needed to keep your house clean. Think about the rules you have to follow outside your home. Maybe signs in your neighborhood tell you not to litter. Maybe there is a crossing guard on the way to school. The crossing guard lets you know when to cross the street. These rules are for your safety and health. You might get sick or injured without them.

Your parent or guardian probably makes the rules that you follow at home. The legislative branch makes the laws that all Americans have to follow. The United States government has three branches. One is the legislative branch. The other two are the executive and judicial

The legislative branch meets in the
United States Capitol building.

branches. The U.S. government follows a process. It starts
with the legislative branch. The legislative branch suggests
and makes laws. The executive branch can either approve

or turn down those laws.
The judicial branch
makes sure these laws are
fair. The executive and
judicial branches need the
legislative branch to do
their jobs.

It takes a lot of people
to make laws. There are
535 people in the U.S.
government who make
laws. The executive branch
can come up with ideas for
laws. But the legislative

THE VOTING RIGHTS ACT

On March 7, 1965, a group of more than 500 black men and women marched into Selma, Alabama. They thought they should have the right to vote. They weren't carrying any weapons. But police still attacked them. Video of the event shocked some members of the legislative branch. They decided to take action. The Voting Rights Act was passed in August 1965. This act finally gave black people the right to vote.

branch can vote against them. The legislative branch makes
the United States different from many other countries.
Executive branches in other countries make laws. Their
legislative branches don't have the power to refuse them.
But all three branches work together in the United States.

Making laws for an entire country is no easy task.
The legislative branch works hard to make laws that help

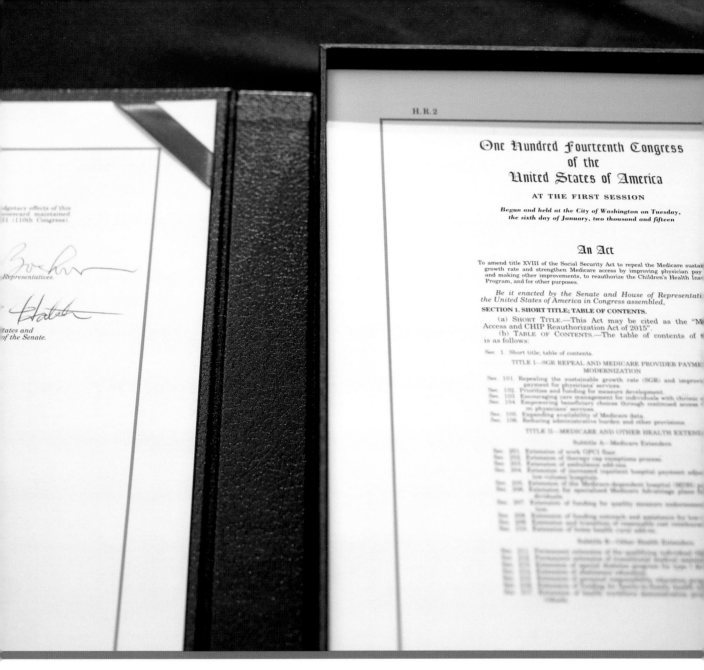

Many laws help protect the health, safety, and rights of Americans.

the American people. The laws that the legislative branch make now will affect Americans in the future.

CHAPTER 2

WHAT IS CONGRESS?

Congress makes up the legislative branch. There are two groups in Congress. These two groups work together to make laws. One group is the Senate. Members of the Senate are called senators. There are 100 senators in the Senate. People living in each state elect their senators. Senators represent the interests of their states in Congress. Each state has two senators.

The other group is the House of Representatives. It is made up of 435 representatives. People living in each state also elect their representatives. But each state does not have the same number of representatives. That number depends on a state's population. Rhode Island is the smallest U.S. state. It has two representatives. Alaska is the biggest U.S. state. But Alaska has only one representative. Alaska has more land area than any other state. But it has one of the smallest populations. California is the state with the highest population. More than 38 million people live in

The House of Representatives meets in its own room in the U.S. Capitol building. The room was first used in 1857.

California. California has 53 representatives. That is more than any other state.

Senators serve six-year **terms**. The U.S. Constitution doesn't limit a senator's number of terms. Each senator has to be reelected at the end of his or her six-year term. Every two years, one-third of the senators are up for reelection. This keeps all senators from being up for election at once.

Eager Street Academy #884
401 East Eager Street
Baltimore, MD 21202

Representatives each serve two-year terms. The Constitution also doesn't limit the number of terms that a representative can serve. But all representatives face reelection every two years. The government looks at the number of representatives per state every ten years. Some states might grow in population. These states might be given more representatives. The populations in some states might shrink. These states might lose representatives.

Each representative belongs to a political party. Political parties are groups of people with similar ideas and beliefs. The U.S. government has a multi-party system. But there are two main political parties: Democrats and Republicans. Whichever party has the most representatives in both the House and Senate is called the majority party. The party with fewer representatives is called the minority party.

The Senate and the House each has its own leader. The vice president acts as head of the Senate. His or her official title is President of the Senate. Sometimes a **bill** is tied in the Senate. The vice president can cast the deciding vote to break the tie.

The Speaker of the House acts as head of the House. Majority party members elect the Speaker. He or she

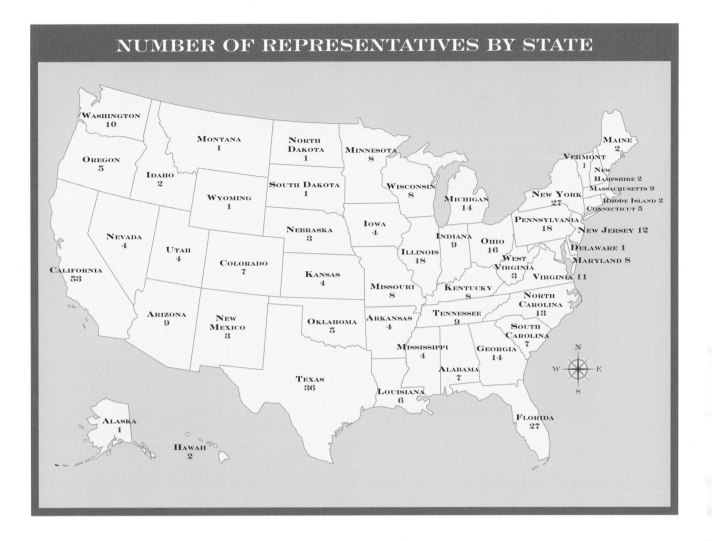

leads debates in the House. The Speaker also talks directly
with the president. The Speaker is second in line for
the presidency. The Speaker would become president
if something happened to both the president and the
vice president.

Congress has other important jobs besides making laws.
The president has the power to **appoint** people to his or
her cabinet. A cabinet is a group of advisers. The president

Paul Ryan became Speaker of the House in 2015.

also can appoint justices to the Supreme Court. The Supreme Court is the main body within the judicial branch. Congress can accept or turn down the president's choices. Congress also has the power to send the country to war. The president needs the help of Congress to accomplish many of his or her duties.

WOMEN IN CONGRESS

The first woman in Congress was elected in 1916. That was four years before women won the right to vote. But women made up fewer than 3 percent of Congress before 1992. The number of women elected to Congress doubled in 1992. That year was called the "Year of the Woman." There were 24 women elected to the House and four elected to the Senate.

CHAPTER 3

THE HISTORY OF THE LEGISLATIVE BRANCH

The 13 American colonies fought the American Revolution from 1775 to 1783. They wanted to break free from Great Britain and King George III. The colonists worked to create a new government. Colonists thought the central government had too much power under a king. Colonists didn't want a strong central government. They wanted to give each of the colonies more power. **Delegates** from each colony except Rhode Island formed the Second Continental Congress. The Continental Congress wrote the Articles of Confederation in 1776. The colonies later were called states. All 13 states approved the Articles of Confederation by 1781. They were the rules of law from 1781 until 1789. The legislative branch was the only branch of government.

The Articles of Confederation put Congress in charge of the government. Members of Congress had many tasks. They were responsible for borrowing money. They

The U.S. Constitution is four pages long. It is on display in Washington, DC.

controlled the postal service and could ask for military troops. But Congress didn't have enough power to complete all of these tasks. The Articles of Confederation gave states more power than Congress. But they created a central government that was too weak. Congress knew that changes needed to be made.

Congress wrote the U.S. Constitution in 1787. It created three branches of government. Delegates knew that Congress had to be more powerful for it to be effective. But they didn't want it to become too powerful. They decided to separate government tasks. The government was split into the legislative, executive, and judicial branches. Each branch would make sure the other branches didn't have

Delegates wrote the Constitution in
Philadelphia, Pennsylvania.

too much power. This is known as a checks-and-balances
system.

Delegates also created a checks-and-balances system
within the legislative branch. The legislative branch was
unicameral under the Articles of Confederation. It had
only one chamber. Delegates thought a one-chamber
Congress would grow too powerful. They decided to create
a **bicameral** system. They split Congress into two chambers.
This would allow one chamber to check the power of the
other. The two chambers were the Senate and the House of
Representatives.

THE THREE BRANCHES OF GOVERNMENT

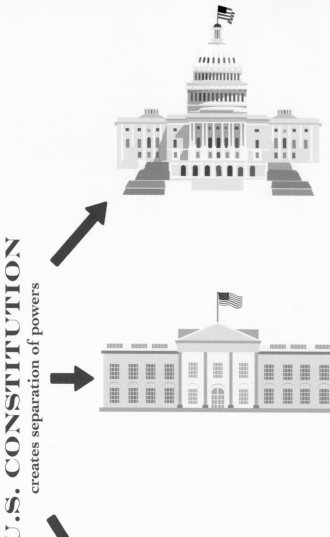

U.S. CONSTITUTION
creates separation of powers

LEGISLATIVE BRANCH
makes laws

CONGRESS

Senate
- 100 senators

House of Representatives
- 435 representatives

EXECUTIVE BRANCH
approves laws

PRESIDENT

Vice President
Cabinet

JUDICIAL BRANCH
makes sure laws are fair

SUPREME COURT
- 9 justices

Other federal courts

The first House and Senate were elected in 1789. There were fewer than four million people living in the United States at that time. There were only 13 states. The first Senate had 26 senators. The first House had 65 members. But the U.S. population grew quickly. Citizens needed more people to represent them, and Congress grew. Then a law was made in 1911. It limited the number of representatives to 435 members.

There are more than 300 million people living in the United States today. Congress tries to represent the interests of all of them. The size of the legislative branch has changed over the years. But its purpose has not. Congress still makes laws that help the country function smoothly.

MAKING FAIR LAWS

The legislative branch faces many problems. It tries to make fair laws for all Americans. But some laws reflect the common beliefs of a certain time in history. These beliefs sometimes discriminated against certain groups of people. This meant some laws were unfair to some people. But some laws have given people more rights. One was the 19th Amendment in 1920. This gave women the right to vote. The legislative branch also passed the Americans with Disabilities Act in 1990. This law made the lives of disabled people better.

CHAPTER 4

THE LEGISLATIVE PROCESS

Legislators have an important job. Representatives and senators work together to make bills into laws. This is called the legislative process.

The first step in the legislative process is writing a bill. Bills start with an idea for a new law. Legislators aren't the only people who can write bills. The president or people in other branches can also write bills. But only a representative can present the bill in Congress. One or more representatives **sponsor** the bill. They try to get people in Congress to support it.

Then the bill is sent to a **committee** in the House of Representatives. Each committee is responsible for a certain part of government, such as money and education. Legislators look over the bill to decide which committee to send it to. There are 20 Senate committees and 23 House committees.

The House votes on bills using electronic voting machines. Pressing "Yea" approves a bill, while "Nay" opposes it.

Members of the House committee talk about a bill first. The committee looks for any changes a bill might need. Members vote to accept or turn down these changes. The committee then votes on the bill. The bill moves on to the House if it is approved. Then the entire House votes on the bill. A bill needs at least 218 of 435 representatives to vote to approve it. Then the bill moves on to a Senate committee.

The Senate committee talks about the bill. It may make changes to the bill. Then the Senate votes on the bill. The bill must be approved by at least 51 of the 100 senators. Then it moves on to the next step.

After the House, a bill is passed on to
one of 20 Senate committees.

House and Senate members make up a conference committee. The House and Senate each created a form of the bill. The conference committee looks at both forms. The conference committee works out any differences or changes needed. Then a final bill is sent to both the House and the Senate for approval.

Then the final bill is sent to the president. The president signs the bill into law if he or she agrees with it. But the president may disagree with the bill. He or she has the power to **veto** a bill. The president must veto the bill within ten days. The bill becomes law if the president waits ten days or more to decide.

HOW A BILL BECOMES LAW

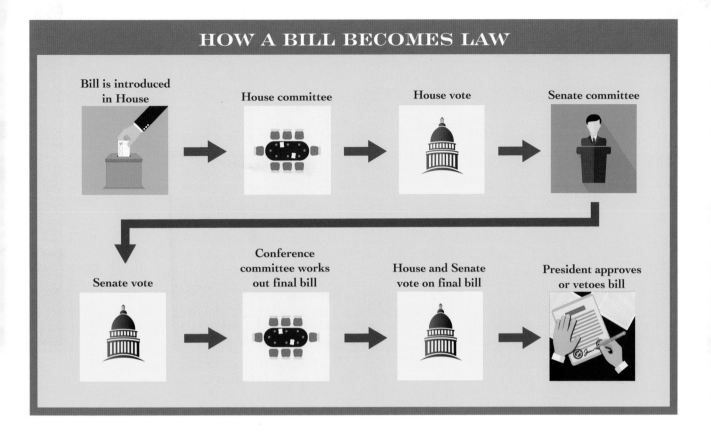

Bill is introduced in House → House committee → House vote → Senate committee → Senate vote → Conference committee works out final bill → House and Senate vote on final bill → President approves or vetoes bill

A veto doesn't always end the legislative process. Congress has the power to stop the president's veto. The Senate and the House can vote to stop a veto. Two-thirds of Congress must vote to block it. The bill becomes law if this happens.

The legislative process might seem long and challenging. The founders of the Constitution made it this way on purpose. This system makes sure a bill is as strong as possible. The legislative process helps Congress make old laws better. It also helps create new, fairer laws for the future.

amendment (uh-MEND-ment) An amendment is an addition or change to a document. The 19th Amendment gave women the right to vote.

appoint (ah-POINT) To appoint is to choose someone for a job. The president can appoint people to the cabinet and the Supreme Court.

bicameral (bye-KAM-ur-ul) Something that is bicameral has two parts. The legislative branch is bicameral because it is made up of the Senate and the House of Representatives.

bill (BIL) A bill is a written plan for a new law. Congress decides if a bill should become a law.

committee (kuh-MIT-ee) A committee is a group of people who discuss topics and make decisions for a larger group. The Senate and House conference committee comes up with the final bill.

delegates (DEL-i-gits) Delegates are people who represent a place or group. Delegates from every state but Rhode Island planned the Constitution.

discriminated (diss-KRIM-uh-nate-id) To be discriminated against is to be treated unfairly. Some laws have discriminated against certain groups of people.

legislators (LEJ-is-ley-torz) Legislators are people who make laws. Members of the U.S. Congress are legislators.

sponsor (SPON-sur) To sponsor is to give support to someone or something. Representatives sponsor bills that they believe should be made into laws.

terms (TURMZ) Terms are set periods of time. Senators have six-year terms.

unicameral (yoo-nuh-KAM-ur-ul) Something that is unicameral has only one part. The legislative branch was unicameral before the U.S. Constitution was written.

veto (VEE-toh) To veto means to stop a bill from becoming a law. The president can veto a bill.

TO LEARN MORE

IN THE LIBRARY

Bow, James. *What Is the Legislative Branch?*
New York: Crabtree Publishing Company, 2013.

Cummings, Matthew. *What Is the Legislative Branch?*
New York: Rosen Publishing, 2015.

Murcia, Rebecca Thatcher. *The Legislative Branch.*
Hockessin, DE: Mitchell Lane Publishers, 2012.

Sobel, Syl. *How the U.S. Government Works.* Hauppauge, NY: Barron's, 2012.

ON THE WEB

Visit our Web site for links about the legislative branch: **childsworld.com/links**

Note to Parents, Teachers, and Librarians: We routinely verify our Web links to make
sure they are safe and active sites. So encourage your readers to check them out!

INDEX

ABOUT THE AUTHOR

Maddie Spalding is an enthusiastic writer and reader. She lives in Minneapolis, Minnesota. Her favorite part of writing is learning about new and interesting subjects.

BOOK CHARGING CARD

Accession No. _____ Call No. _____

Author_____

Title_____

Date Loaned	Borrower's Name	Date Re...